Confessing Our Sins

GW00808907

Andrew Atherstone

Curate, Christ Church, Abingdon

GROVE BOOKS LIMITED
RIDLEY HALL RD CAMBRIDGE CB3 9HU

Contents

Acknowledgments

I am grateful to members of GROW (the Group for the Renewal of Worship) for their comments on a draft of this booklet, in particular to Christopher Byworth, Anna de Lange, Mark Earey, Anne Harrison, Charles Read and Tim Stratford. Bible quotations are taken from the New International Version.

The Cover Illustration is by Peter Ashton

First Impression April 2004
ISSN 0144-1728
ISBN 1 85174 559 9

Introduction

Confession of our sins to God is one of the key aspects of Christian worship.

It is part of the regular Sunday routine of most church-goers. Models of public worship frequently include it as an essential element—for example, ACTS (adoration, confession, thanksgiving, supplication) or the Four Ps (praise, penitence, proclamation, petition) or the Four Cs (confession, celebration, call, commitment). And yet very often our corporate confession can be humdrum and bland, a part of worship merely to be endured. We go through the motions out of habit but often find it unstimulating and of little spiritual benefit. Furthermore an emphasis on sin seems unattractive, especially off-putting to non-Christian visitors. We prefer praise to lament, cheerful up-beat worship to mournful penitence. As a result some congregations keep confession to the bare minimum or give it up altogether. Is corporate confession really essential? What does the Bible say on the subject? How can prayers of penitence be revitalized as an engaging and profitable part of our worship? What should be considered when writing or choosing penitential material? What are the theological strengths and weaknesses of the confessions and absolutions in *Common Worship*? What can we learn from the priorities of the first Anglican Reformers? What about the use of symbolism? This booklet aims to explore these issues.

Biblical Principles

Throughout its pages, the Bible treats sin with deadly seriousness. Sin is rebellion against God. It is detestable to him and separates us from him. Scripture explains that all have rebelled and therefore all are guilty before God and facing his holy wrath. Sin brings sorrow and suffering to many people in this life and irretrievable ruin to some in the next.

This is the heart of the glorious Christian gospel—it is good news indeed

Thankfully the Bible does not stop with that stark diagnosis. It goes on to explain that no matter how terrible our sins, forgiveness can be obtained through the sin-bearing death of Jesus Christ, the saviour of the world. This is the heart of the glorious Christian gospel—it is good news indeed. As the apostle Paul explains to Timothy: 'Here is a trustworthy saying that deserves full acceptance: Christ Jesus came into the world to save sinners' (1 Timothy 1.15). Salvation is found when we repent of our wrongdoing and put our faith in Christ.

The call to repent was a central part of Jesus' teaching during his earthly ministry (Matthew 4.17) and was reiterated by his apostles. For instance, Peter told a crowd in Jerusalem, 'Repent and turn to God, so that your sins may be wiped out…' (Acts 3.19). Likewise Paul told King Agrippa that wherever he went around the Roman Empire he exhorted people to repent and turn to God and prove their repentance by their deeds (Acts 26.20). In the apostolic message, the call to repent and the call to believe in the Lord Jesus are inseparably linked.

Repentance means much more than just 'saying sorry.' Rightly understood, it means to turn away from sin and turn to God, with all the radical transformation in attitude and actions that such a momentous change entails. James Packer usefully summarizes the process of repentance as follows:

- realistic recognition that one has disobeyed and failed God
- regretful remorse at the dishonour one has done to God
- reverent requesting of God's pardon, cleansing of conscience, and help not to lapse in the same way again
- resolute renunciation of the sins in question, with deliberate thought of how to keep clear of them and live right for the future
- requisite restitution to any who have suffered material loss through one's wrongdoing.[1]

Confession, then, is a natural part of repentance. Yet is it an essential part? Although there are hundreds of examples in the Bible of people repenting, there is surprisingly little about them confessing. Is this practice really so important? After all, we are justified by faith not by confession.

The importance of confession is made clear by Jesus' model of prayer for his disciples, which includes the petition, 'Forgive us our sins' (Luke 11.4). Furthermore, a number of Jesus' parables connect repentance and confession. For example, the prodigal son comes to his senses, distressed at his mistakes, and returns to his father with the words, 'Father, I have sinned against heaven and against you. I am no longer worthy to be called your son' (Luke 15.17–21). Similarly, the tax collector praying next to the Pharisee in the temple beats his breast and cries out, 'God, have mercy on me, a sinner' (Luke 18.9–14).

The importance of confession is made clear by Jesus' model of prayer

Other passages in the Bible show that confession is a natural part of the life of God's people. Indeed it is essential to our spiritual vitality, as the wise sayings of Solomon point out: 'He who conceals his sins does not prosper, but whoever confesses and renounces them finds mercy' (Proverbs 28.13). The prophet Hosea exhorts his listeners:

> Return, O Israel, to the Lord your God.
> Your sins have been your downfall!
> Take words with you and return to the Lord.
> Say to him: 'Forgive all our sins and receive us graciously,
> that we may offer the fruit of our lips.' (Hosea 14.1–2)

Likewise the apostle John instructs his congregations to confess their sins, that they may be forgiven and purified by God (1 John 1.9). Several of the psalms give examples of confession, most famously Psalm 51, composed by David after his adultery with Bathsheba was discovered. At the time of the exile, Daniel fasted in sackcloth and ashes and confessed to God the sins of the Israelites (Daniel 9.1–19). Nehemiah also wept, fasted and confessed the people's sins, including those of himself and his family (Nehemiah 1.4–11). Job's confession after his confrontation with God is briefly recorded (Job 42.1–6).

Most confession in the Bible is apparently secret, between the sinner and God, but it is also occasionally public. Under the sacrificial system set up by Moses, the guilty party not only had to bring a lamb or goat as a sin offering so that the priest might make atonement, but was also required to confess openly the nature of his wrongdoing (Leviticus 5.5–6, see also Numbers 5.5–7). On Yom Kippur, the annual Day of Atonement, Aaron laid his hands on the scapegoat and confessed over it all the wickedness of the people before it was banished to the desert (Leviticus 16.20–22). Old Testament prophets not only denounced the sins of the nation, but also sometimes publicly confessed them. For instance, Isaiah lamented:

> Our offences are many in your sight,
>   and our sins testify against us.
> Our offences are ever with us,
>   and we acknowledge our iniquities...   (Isaiah 59.12)
>
> Do not be angry beyond measure, O Lord;
>   do not remember our sins for ever.
> O, look upon us we pray,
>   for we are all your people.   (Isaiah 64.9)

Similar examples are found in the New Testament. When John the Baptist exhorted the Judean crowds to 'Repent, for the kingdom of heaven is near,' they responded by confessing their sins before being baptized in the River Jordan (Matthew 3.1–6, Mark 1.4–5). During Paul's mission to Ephesus, many of the new believers openly confessed their evil practices, while those who had been involved in sorcery burnt their scrolls for all to see (Acts 19.17–20). In these instances, public confession appears to have been largely spontaneous, spoken out by individuals in different ways as befitting their various circumstances.

Corporate Confession?

Only on a very few occasions does the Bible give explicit examples of *corporate* confession of sin. When the Israelites were being oppressed by their Philistine neighbours, the prophet Samuel instructed them to return to the Lord with all their hearts and serve him only. So the people destroyed their false gods and met together in a great assembly at Mizpah, where they fasted and confessed their apostasy: 'We have sinned against the Lord' (1 Samuel 7.2–6, 12.10). Centuries later, when the Jewish remnant had returned from exile in Babylon, they gathered together in a large assembly, led by the Levites, to confess their sins and worship God. This was combined with Bible reading and fasting, performed in sackcloth and ashes (Nehemiah 9). On another occasion Ezra was appalled to discover that those returning had begun to intermarry with neighbouring people groups and adopt their 'detestable' religious practices. So he pulled out his hair, tore his clothes and prostrated himself before the Lord at the evening sacrifice, confessing the people's sins. A large crowd of Israelites gathered around, including women and children, and joined Ezra in his bitter weeping (Ezra 9.1–10.1). Other instances of corporate confession may be inferred. For example, the seven penitential psalms (Psalms 6, 32, 38, 51, 102, 130, 143) were probably used, like the rest of the psalter, as a resource for Israel's congregational worship.

Corporate confession is a way of expressing publicly the importance of repentance in the Christian life

Although there is biblical precedent for public corporate confession, it is by no means clear that God's people lamented their sins every time they gathered. Rather it is with secret individual confession that the emphasis should lie, as part of our daily devotions. When we become aware of our sin, repentance must be immediate—we do not have to save it up for Sunday morning. Nevertheless, corporate confession will remain a natural and regular part of our worship as we recall the holiness of God. It is a way of expressing publicly the importance of repentance in the Christian life and should be revitalized rather than neglected.

Reformation Revisions

2

No one can read the Book of Common Prayer without noticing its heavy emphasis upon sin.

For example, the baptism service states that we are 'conceived and born in sin,' weddings that marriage is 'a remedy against sin' and funerals that death delivers us 'out of the miseries of this sinful world.' Stress upon the terrible consequences of sin and our need for mercy from God is found particularly in the rites for Morning and Evening Prayer and Holy Communion. One of Thomas Cranmer's most significant liturgical legacies was his strengthening of penitential material in these services. He knew that we cannot grasp the good news about salvation through Christ until we first appreciate the bad news of bondage to sin.

> *We cannot grasp the good news until we first appreciate the bad news of bondage to sin*

Morning and Evening Prayer

During the Middle Ages the Western tradition observed seven 'canonical hours,' but Cranmer reduced the number to just two, renamed 'Morning Prayer' and 'Evening Prayer.' At first these new daily services contained no penitential material, so in 1552 he added a lengthy exhortation, confession and absolution. One of Cranmer's motives in making this change was to avoid the need for private 'auricular' confession which had become widespread in the medieval church. The opening declaration explains that 'although we ought at all times humbly to acknowledge our sins before God; yet ought we most chiefly so to do, when we assemble and meet together…' This was an attempt to bring confession out of the priest's booth and back into the public domain. Cranmer intended sins to be corporately confessed twice a day every day, although in the new *Common Worship* daily office this is optional. Under the provisions of 'A Service of the Word,' confession is now only compulsory on Sundays and principal holy days (Ash Wednesday, Maundy Thursday and Good Friday), and then only at the 'principal service.'

Holy Communion

The Lord's Supper, as revised by Cranmer, had a much stronger penitential flavour than the Latin Mass. It was stripped of its elaborate rituals, no longer a feast for the senses. Gorgeous coloured vestments, flower decorations and the sweet smell of incense were abolished. There was no longer any singing, except for *Gloria in excelsis*. With these omissions came several corresponding penitential additions, such as an extended confession and the new Prayer of Humble Access.

In typical Reformed fashion, Cranmer inserted three lengthy exhortations into his liturgy, which passed with some alteration into the 1662 Prayer Book. The first is a general warning about the seriousness of Holy Communion. It explains that we are in 'great peril' of 'damnation' if we receive the sacrament unworthily. Therefore confession of sin is vital before approaching the Lord's Table and the congregation is exhorted

> to examine your lives and conversations by the rule of God's commandments; and whereinsoever ye shall perceive yourselves to have offended, either by will, word, or deed, there to bewail your own sinfulness, and to confess yourselves to Almighty God, with full purpose of amendment of life...Therefore if any of you be a blasphemer of God, an hinderer or slanderer of his Word, an adulterer, or be in malice, or envy, or in any other grievous crime, repent you of your sins, or else come not to that holy Table...

The third exhortation, addressed to those actually about to receive communion, is similar in tone. It outlines the importance of self-examination and confession before the Lord's Supper to ensure we receive the sacrament 'with a true penitent heart and lively faith.'

Despite Cranmer's efforts to encourage frequent reception of communion, many church-goers only attended the Ante-communion. Indeed if there were not enough communicants, the whole service had to stop soon after the homily, which meant missing out the exhortation, confession and absolution. It was thus possible to attend church without ever having seriously to consider one's sins. To get around this difficulty, Cranmer increased the penitential material even further in 1552 by adding the Ten Commandments at the start of the service, with the ancient *kyrie* formula adapted as a response to each commandment. *Common Worship* maintains Cranmer's service structure in Order Two of Holy Communion. However, the sixteenth century problem of people only attending Ante-communion is no longer an issue today. Therefore the more popular Order One gathers the penitential material together, usually at the start of the service (following the pattern of the Roman rite).

Unlike Cranmer's Prayer Book, *Common Worship* allows flexibility in the position of the prayers of penitence.[2] Great variety is now possible. For example, confession may take place

- before the opening hymn—perhaps at the start of Advent or Lent
- after the opening hymn—as a precursor to the body of the service
- after the Bible readings—drawing out penitential material in a reading
- after the sermon—in response to God's Word
- during the intercessions—as part of praying for the world
- before the Lord's Supper—recalling the benefits of Christ's death

Wherever they are said, the prayers of penitence have four key components—preparation, invitation, confession, absolution—each of which we shall consider in turn.

Preparing to Confess 3

When asked how long he prayed each day, Archbishop Michael Ramsey is reputed to have said he prayed for only two minutes.

At the questioner's obvious surprise, the archbishop explained: 'I spend 28 minutes getting ready and two minutes praying!'[3] Proper preparation is vital. If this is true before worship in general, it is especially so before confession.

Too easily we hurry into confession without stopping to reflect. We arrive at church on a Sunday morning in a rush, after a busy week. After the opening hymn we kneel down and confess our sins in thirty seconds flat, with a form of words we know by rote, before the service moves quickly on. Our confession is typically of the 'omnibus' variety: 'O God, I'm sorry for my sins, Amen.' Perhaps we acknowledge that we have sinned 'in thought, word and deed,' but week after week goes by without time to consider which of our thoughts, words and deeds have actually been sinful.

Confession is of greatest benefit when it is detailed. As the Prayer of Preparation states, we approach 'Almighty God, to whom all hearts are open, all desires known, and from whom no secrets are hidden.' God searches our hearts and we should do likewise. The spiritual discipline of self-examination has fallen into wide disuse, but the church would greatly benefit from its rediscovery. One of the main reasons we make such slow progress on the path to holiness is that we fail to identify our specific sins or seek the Holy Spirit's aid in overcoming them. Self-examination should be a regular part of our private devotions, but is also important in corporate worship.[4] Opportunity for such preparation may be provided by the use of extended silence, reading of Scripture or a suitable song. *Common Worship* also offers 'A Form of Preparation' (pp 161–165) which may be used privately by individuals before the service or as part of the service itself.

It is often as we meditate upon God's Word that God's Spirit convicts us of our sin. Therefore *Common Worship* recommends the following four selections of Bible verses to aid our preparation:

- **The Ten Commandments** These may be used in several forms, perhaps adding a positive New Testament instruction after the Commandments' prohibition. For example, 'You shall not commit murder. Live peaceably with all; overcome evil with good… You shall not commit adultery. Know that your body is a temple of the Holy Spirit…You shall not steal. Be honest in all that you do, and care for those in need.' (*CW*, pp 270–271)
- **A Summary of the Law** The Non-jurors first used a summary of the law, from Matthew 22.37–40, for their communion liturgy of 1718. The version in *Common Worship* is taken mainly from Mark 12.29–31.
- **The Beatitudes**
- **The Comfortable Words** These Bible promises about the work of Jesus Christ were originally attached to the absolution and would best be returned there (see discussion below). Although they rightly reassure us that we will be forgiven if we turn to Christ, they do not reveal specific areas in which we have fallen short of his demands, unlike the Ten Commandments or the Beatitudes.

Many other parts of the Bible bring us face to face with God's righteous standards, such as the teaching on holy living in the New Testament letters (for example, Romans 12.9–21, 1 Corinthians 13.1–7, Galatians 5.16–25, Colossians 3.1–14, James 3.13–18, 2 Peter 1.3–11). Meditation on these passages is valuable during self-examination before confession.

Invitation to Confess 4

The invitation to confession is usually just a few words said by the worship leader.

It may seem so obvious as not to require discussion here. In fact, however, it repays careful thought. When neglected, the invitation becomes perfunctory and is sometimes reduced to a barren stage direction: 'Now let's say the confession together.' Yet it has rich potential, when considered in advance, to help us focus on why and how we should confess.

The Prayer Book services of Morning and Evening Prayer begin with the minister reading penitential sentences from the Bible and exhorting the congregation:

> Dearly beloved brethren, the Scripture moveth us in sundry places to acknowledge and confess our manifold sins and wickedness; and that we should not dissemble nor cloke them before the face of Almighty God our heavenly Father; but confess them with an humble, lowly, penitent, and obedient heart; to the end that we may obtain forgiveness of the same, by his infinite goodness and mercy...

The congregation is then invited to approach 'with a pure heart, and humble voice, unto the throne of the heavenly grace.' As one writer has put it, this exhortation is designed 'to instruct the ignorant, to admonish the negligent, to support the fearful, to comfort the doubtful, to caution the formal, and to check the presumptuous—tempers which are found in every mixed congregation.'[5] It contains three important themes:

- the biblical injunction to confess
- the right attitude of confession—humble, penitent, obedient, honest
- the character of God—he is almighty and seated on a royal throne, but is also a heavenly Father, of infinite goodness and mercy, gracious and ready to forgive

It is worthwhile considering these principles when choosing (or writing) an invitation to confession. In *Common Worship* the standard exhortation at Morning and Evening Prayer is now:

> Jesus says, 'Repent, for the kingdom of heaven is close at hand.' So let us turn away from our sin and turn to Christ, confessing our sins in penitence and faith.

This includes two of the three themes from the above model. It has a penitential sentence from the Bible and tells us about the right attitude of confession, but says nothing about the character of Christ. Further suggestions are offered in *Common Worship* (pp 300–328) and *New Patterns for Worship* (pp 77–80). A weak example, which includes none of the above themes, is the sparse instruction:

> Brothers and sisters, as we prepare to celebrate, let us call to mind our sins. (NPW, p 77)

A more weighty example, which includes all three elements of Cranmer's model, is:

> The sacrifice of God is a broken spirit; a broken and contrite heart God will not despise. Let us come to the Lord, who is full of compassion, and acknowledge our transgressions in penitence and faith.
>
> (CW, p 308; compare Psalm 51.17)

The invitation to confession may be composed by local worship leaders to emphasize the main theme of a service. Penitential material from the Bible readings may be drawn out, perhaps introduced with words such as 'The Psalmist says…' or 'Isaiah prophesies…' or 'The Apostle Paul writes…' Particular aspects of God's character may be stressed, always remembering that we will more readily approach God when told not just of his holiness and judgment but also his mercy and readiness to forgive.

Confession

5

The archaic language of the Prayer Book confessions sounds unintelligible, even humorous, to modern ears.

It has led to the tired joke about miserable Anglicans in their miserable churches. These confessions are also criticized for being wordy and didactic. Nonetheless they still provide us with a valuable model with which to compare those in *Common Worship*. Therefore we shall first study the Prayer Book confessions, identifying their key theological themes.

At Morning and Evening Prayer, the confession reads as follows:

> Almighty and most merciful Father,
> we have erred and strayed from thy ways like lost sheep.
> We have followed too much the devices and desires of our own hearts.
> We have offended against thy holy laws.
> We have left undone those things which we ought to have done;
> and we have done those things which we ought not to have done;
> and there is no health in us.
> But thou, O Lord, have mercy upon us, miserable offenders.
> Spare thou them, O God, which confess their faults.
> Restore thou them that are penitent;
> according to thy promises declared unto mankind in Christ Jesu our Lord.
> And grant, O most merciful Father, for his sake,
> that we may hereafter live a godly, righteous, and sober life,
> to the glory of thy holy name.
> Amen.

The confession at Holy Communion is similar in nature:

> Almighty God,
> Father of our Lord Jesus Christ,
> maker of all things, judge of all men:
> we acknowledge and bewail our manifold sins and wickedness,
> which we, from time to time, most grievously have committed,
> by thought, word, and deed,

against thy Divine Majesty,
provoking most justly thy wrath and indignation against us.
We do earnestly repent,
and are heartily sorry for these our misdoings;
the remembrance of them is grievous unto us;
the burden of them is intolerable.
Have mercy upon us,
have mercy upon us, most merciful Father;
for thy Son our Lord Jesus Christ's sake,
forgive us all that is past;
and grant that we may ever hereafter
serve and please thee in newness of life,
to the honour and glory of thy name;
through Jesus Christ our Lord.
Amen.

Both confessions are phrased in corporate language ('we acknowledge...we repent...forgive us') and include a number of important themes:

- **the character of God**—he is our creator, a just judge, a holy king, the lawgiver, a God of wrath, but also a merciful Father
- **the promises of Jesus**—we ask forgiveness in his name
- **the nature of sin**—it means breaking God's laws, straying from God's ways, following our own desires, sinning by commission and omission in thought, word and deed. These are both 'general' confessions, as opposed to the particular confession that might be made by an individual in secret. No mention is made of specific offences, such as flirting with the next-door-neighbour or misleading the Inland Revenue or drinking too much at the pub last Friday. Instead the sins described are 'general' ones that everybody commits every day.
- **the seriousness of sin**—our sins are 'intolerable' (that is, too heavy to bear); there is no 'health' (that is, salvation) in ourselves, but only God can save; we are 'miserable' (that is, to be pitied)
- **lament**—we 'bewail' our sins, even the memory of which is painful; we approach God in sorrow and penitence
- **prayer for pardon for the past**—for mercy and restoration
- **prayer for grace for the future**—that we may live holy lives
- **the glory of God as our ultimate aim**

Conspicuous by its absence, when compared with other Calvinist liturgies, is any explicit mention of the corruption of our human nature. For example,

Hermann of Weid's *Simple and Religious Consultation* (1547), which Cranmer largely followed, includes the phrase, 'we lament that we were conceived and born in sins, and that therefore we be prone to all evils.' Although Cranmer and the other Anglican Reformers believed in 'original' sin (see Article IX), these Prayer Book confessions do not highlight it lest we think we have an excuse for our wrongdoing. The declaration that 'there is no health in us' may be seen as a hint but it is no more than that.

There are now at least 22 authorized forms of confession in modern English, scattered throughout *Common Worship* and brought together in *New Patterns for Worship* (pp 81–90). Some stick closely to the old Prayer Book confessions, updating the language. Others are recent compositions from various sources.[6] Some are to be said by the whole congregation, others are responsive. Each repays careful comparison with the above principles in order to weigh its various theological strengths and weaknesses. Unfortunately space permits us to examine only three here.

---

1   God of mercy,
    we acknowledge that we are all sinners.
    We turn from the wrong that we have thought and said and done,
    and are mindful of all that we have failed to do.
    For the sake of Jesus, who died for us,
    forgive us for all that is past,
    and help us to live each day
    in the light of Christ our Lord.
    Amen.

This confession is strong at praying for pardon for the past and grace for the future. It explicitly mentions the prevalence of sin ('we are all sinners') and the death of Jesus for our sake. However, the character of God is barely mentioned (apart from his mercy) and there is no lament at the seriousness of sin (the weak phrase 'are mindful' fails to capture any real sense of concern). The fact that we have sinned against God is not made explicit.

---

2   Father,
    we have sinned against heaven and against you.
    We are not worthy to be called your children.
    We turn to you again.
    Have mercy on us,
    bring us back to yourself
    as those who once were dead
    but now have life through Christ our Lord.
    Amen.

This confession contains a healthy note of lament ('we are not worthy'). It points out the seriousness of sin ('once dead') and the fact that life comes through Christ. The character of God is briefly mentioned (a merciful Father). However, the prayer does not explain in what ways we have sinned nor does it ask for future grace. Although the phrase 'against heaven and against you' is taken from the prodigal son's appeal to his human father, it is bizarre here since our Father to whom we pray is in heaven.

3   Lord God, our maker and our redeemer,
    this is your world and we are your people:
    come among us and save us.

    We have wilfully misused your gifts of creation;
    Lord, be merciful: **forgive us our sin.**

    We have seen the ill-treatment of others
    and have not gone to their aid;
    Lord, be merciful: **forgive us our sin.**

    We have condoned evil and dishonesty
    and failed to strive for justice;
    Lord, be merciful: **forgive us our sin.**

    We have heard the good news of Christ,
    but have failed to share it with others;
    Lord, be merciful: **forgive us our sin.**

    We have not loved you with all our heart,
    nor our neighbours as ourselves:
    Lord, be merciful: **forgive us our sin.**

This confession is strong on the character of God (he is our creator, merciful redeemer, Lord and Saviour). Like most of the responsive confessions in *Common Worship* it is also good at expanding upon the nature of our sins, rather than the catch-all 'by thought, word and deed.' These concrete, but still general, examples help us to be better focused and make powerful connections with corporate societal sin (an obvious lack in the Prayer Book confessions). However, there is no petition for future grace, while the seriousness of sin and the saving work of Christ are not mentioned.

Each of the *Common Worship* confessions has different valuable strengths. Each also has different theological weaknesses. It is therefore worthwhile to reflect on them carefully when choosing appropriate liturgy.

Can We Sin Against Our Neighbour?

In the Prayer Book confessions explicit mention of sin against other people is conspicuously absent. We have strayed from God's ways, broken God's laws and offended God's majesty. Yet there is nothing equivalent to the *Common Worship* admission that we have 'sinned against you *and against our neighbour.*' Some argue that we should only speak of 'sin' as something committed against God. Although we can wrong our neighbours or hurt them or trespass against them, we do not sin against them. This is partly a semantic question. For example, the most popular modern translation of the Lord's Prayer pleads, 'Forgive us our sins as we forgive *those who sin against us*' (see *New International Version* translation of Matthew 6.14–15, Luke 11.4). Linguistic purists would prefer to speak here of 'debt' or 'trespass' rather than 'sin.'

Nevertheless, it is true that sin against God and sin against our neighbour are not equivalent. Therefore it is perhaps misleading to roll them into one phrase. Our sins may bring disgrace to ourselves and sorrow or suffering to others, but they are primarily a rebellion against God. Although many of our sins are committed against other people, we confess them to God because they are first and foremost sins against him. This is what King David meant when, having seduced Bathsheba and murdered her husband, he was yet able to pray: 'Against you, you only, have I sinned' (Psalm 51.4).

Common Worship takes into account these two perspectives. Some confessions speak of sinning against our neighbour. Others speak of sinning against God by breaking his commandment to love our neighbour as ourselves.

Kyrie Confessions

The ancient *kyrie* formula (Kyrie eleison—Christe eleison—Kyrie eleison) was adopted by the Reformers for our early English liturgies and survives in various forms in the Prayer Book. In *Common Worship* it may now be used as a confession, with short penitential sentences placed before each petition (see suggestions at CW pp 133–134, 277–278 and NPW pp 91–94). Care should be taken that these sentences are genuinely penitential and match one another in style. For example:

Like Mary at the empty tomb,
we fail to grasp the wonder of your presence.
Lord have mercy. **Lord, have mercy.**

> Like the disciples behind locked doors,
> we are afraid to be seen as your followers.
> Christ have mercy. **Christ, have mercy.**
>
> Like Thomas in the upper room,
> we are slow to believe.
> Lord, have mercy. **Lord, have mercy.** (NPW, p 92)

Kyrie confessions provide an almost infinite variety of options and may be written by local worship leaders to emphasize a particular theme or draw out material from the Bible readings. However, they do not convey the depth of lament provided by other confessions (except, perhaps, when sung), nor do they highlight the character of God, the work of Christ or the seriousness of sin. Therefore kyrie confessions should be used sparingly and not usually within Sunday worship (except, perhaps, occasional All Age Worship). They may also act as a gentle way of encouraging confession amongst those who are seriously sick and find it hard to concentrate, rather than the normal confessions which require greater mental focus.

6 Absolution

Jesus has power to forgive sins, as he demonstrated during his ministry on earth.

Yet the medieval church claimed that he bestowed the same power upon the apostles and their successors (that is, upon ordained 'priests'). For instance, Jesus promised the keys of the kingdom to Simon Peter with the affirmation, 'whatever you bind on earth will be bound in heaven, and whatever you loose on earth will be loosed in heaven' (Matthew 16.19). After the resurrection he told his disciples, 'If you forgive anyone his sins, they are forgiven; if you do not forgive them, they are not forgiven' (John 20.23), words echoed in the Anglican ordinal. Such texts have led some to argue that an ordained minister has the power to absolve sins. This idea is confirmed in the minds of many congregations when the minister stands for the absolution while they all kneel, or when a deacon or lay leader is only allowed to pray for God to have mercy on 'us' instead of on 'you.' In order to guard against this understanding of priesthood, some congregations have now sadly begun to dispense with the absolution altogether.

This is an important and contentious subject, though there is little space to consider it here. It was vigorously debated at the time of the Reformation and during the nineteenth century when proponents of the Oxford Movement and their ritualist successors began to advocate habitual private confession to a priest. The 'ministry of reconciliation' has since become popular in some parts of the Church of England. Yet because of the wide disagreement amongst Anglicans on this subject, it is one of the few remaining areas upon which the church attempts to keep tight liturgical control (along with eucharistic prayers). Despite the great flexibility of *Common Worship*, only authorized forms of confession and absolution may, in theory, be used.

Unlike some of their continental colleagues, Cranmer and the other Anglican Reformers were happy to retain the practice of absolution. However, they understood it in a different way from their Roman Catholic counterparts. The Reformers insisted that authority to 'bind' and 'loose' lay not in the priesthood but in the gospel, not in the words of human ministers but in the Word of God. They understood Jesus' statements about the 'retention' and 'remission' of sins to refer to the substance of the message that the apostles were to preach—in other words, as a mandate to proclaim the forgiveness of sins through the death of Jesus Christ. This injunction, the Reformers argued, is given not just to ministers but indiscriminately to the whole church, linked closely to the Great Commission and the pouring out of the Holy Spirit. This Reformation perspective should be borne in mind when considering the various forms of absolution found in the Prayer Book.[7]

Absolution usually takes one of three liturgical forms:

* **indicative**—the minister absolves those who repent ('I absolve you...')
* **precatory**—the minister prays that God will absolve those who repent ('May Almighty God pardon you...')
* **declaratory**—the minister declares that God absolves those who repent

The **indicative** form of absolution is traditionally used within the Roman Church privately for individuals during the 'ministry of reconciliation.' It survives, somewhat ambiguously, in the Prayer Book service for the Visitation of the Sick: '...by Christ's authority committed to me, I absolve thee from all thy sins...' The Puritans at the Savoy Conference in 1661 wanted this altered to 'I pronounce thee absolved' but the bishops refused. No modern language version has yet been authorized within *Common Worship*, although the following comes close to it:

God, the Father of mercies,
has reconciled the world to himself
through the death and resurrection of his Son, Jesus Christ,
not counting our trespasses against us,
but sending his Holy Spirit
to shed abroad his love among us.
By the ministry of reconciliation
entrusted by Christ to his Church,
receive his pardon and peace
to stand before him in his strength alone,
this day and evermore.

This absolution is authorized not just for use in private with the sick or dying but also in corporate worship, a novel development.

The **precatory** form of absolution is traditionally used within the Roman Church during corporate worship. It was adopted by the Anglican Reformers for the service of Holy Communion, although with two vital alterations. In the Prayer Book it reads as follows:

Almighty God, our heavenly Father,
who of his great mercy hath promised forgiveness of sins
to all them that with hearty repentance and true faith turn unto him;
Have mercy upon you;
pardon and deliver you from all your sins;
confirm and strengthen you in all goodness;
and bring you to everlasting life;
through Jesus Christ our Lord.
Amen.

Although based on the old Latin form, Cranmer added the important clause about forgiveness being dependent on 'hearty repentance and true faith.' The second significant change was to add the 'comfortable words' immediately after the absolution, an idea taken from Hermann's *Consultation*. They are 'comfortable' because they console the wounded conscience by reminding us of the Bible promises about the work of Jesus Christ on which our forgiveness is based:

> Come to me, all who labour and are heavy laden, and I will give you rest. (Matthew 11.28)
>
> God so loved the world that he gave his only-begotten Son, that whoever believes in him should not perish but have eternal life. (John 3.16)
>
> This saying is true, and worthy of full acceptance, that Christ Jesus came into the world to save sinners. (1 Timothy 1.15)
>
> If anyone sins, we have an advocate with the Father, Jesus Christ the righteous; and he is the propitiation for our sins. (1 John 2.1–2)

Unfortunately *Common Worship* has largely reversed Cranmer's two revisions of the Roman model. The 'comfortable words' are now divorced from the absolution and made instead an optional part of the preparation for confession. Fifteen of the sixteen new absolutions authorized in *Common Worship* follow a precatory form, but only two mention the need for true repentance and faith. Instead we have versions such as

> May almighty God have mercy on us,
> forgive us our sins,
> and bring us to everlasting life,
> through Jesus Christ our Lord.
>
> May the God of love and power
> forgive you and free you from your sins,
> heal and strengthen you by his Spirit,
> and raise you to new life in Christ our Lord.

The **declaratory** form of absolution was not known in the medieval church and was first developed by the Reformers. At Morning and Evening Prayer it reads as follows:

> Almighty God, the Father of our Lord Jesus Christ,
> who desireth not the death of a sinner,
> but rather that he may turn from his wickedness, and live;
> and hath given power, and commandment, to his ministers,
> to declare and pronounce to his people, being penitent,
> the absolution and remission of their sins:
> He pardoneth and absolveth all them that truly repent,
> and unfeignedly believe his holy Gospel.
> Wherefore let us beseech him to grant us true repentance,
> and his Holy Spirit,
> that those things may please him, which we do at this present;

and that the rest of our life hereafter may be pure, and holy;
so that at the last we may come to his eternal joy;
through Jesus Christ our Lord.
Amen.

This declaration includes five important themes:

* the mercy of God
* the authority given to God's ministers to pronounce pardon for sins
* God as the one who pardons
* the dependence of that pardon upon true repentance and faith in the gospel
* the need to ask for God's Holy Spirit to give us that true repentance and help us live holy lives

Unfortunately this declaratory form of absolution has ended up in a liturgical cul-de-sac. No such model is provided in *Common Worship* and it has now become standard, even at Morning and Evening Prayer, to use a precatory form instead. Ministers who wish to follow the Reformers' lead here, though in modern English, have no authorized option. A new version might look something like the following:

Almighty God,
who is compassionate and of abundant mercy,
forgives the sins of all those who truly repent and turn to him in faith.
Therefore let us take hold of the gospel promises with confidence,
praising God for the gift of his Son Jesus Christ,
and praying that his Holy Spirit
would daily increase our passion for holiness.

This is a legitimate form of absolution and we would benefit from its rediscovery. It provides great liturgical potential which has yet to be tapped.

Other Penitential Material 7

The Litany

The Litany is no longer widely used and is seldom heard outside an ordination or cathedral service. Indeed it has become a by-word for any tedious recital. However, it provides valuable penitential material. During the Middle Ages litanies were particularly popular during Lent or on rogation days or at times of national emergency. A pattern of Morning Prayer, the Litany and Ante-communion became the staple diet of many Anglican worshippers from the Reformation until the end of the nineteenth century.

As we might expect, Cranmer strengthened the penitential character of the Litany. This emphasis is still present in *Common Worship*, though to a lesser degree. Mention of 'miserable sinners,' 'everlasting damnation' and God's 'wrath' have vanished, but the Litany still includes prayers for deliverance 'from all evil and mischief; from pride, vanity and hypocrisy; from envy, hatred and malice; and from all evil intent…from sloth, worldliness and love of money; from hardness of heart and contempt for your word and your laws…from sins of body and mind; from the deceits of the world, the flesh and the devil…' The Litany deserves wider use, not just as a substitute for the normal intercessions. Sections I, II, III and VII would well suit any penitential context.

Can We Sin in Ignorance?

The *Common Worship* Litany ends with the following petition:

> Give us true repentance;
> forgive us our sins of negligence and ignorance
> and our deliberate sins;
> and grant us the grace of your Holy Spirit
> to amend our lives according to your holy word.

This is based on Cranmer's prayer for forgiveness from 'all our sins, negligences, and ignorances.' Nevertheless, some argue that if we break God's law unwittingly then we are not counted guilty of sin. In Series 3 the confession at Holy Communion spoke of sin 'through

---

ignorance, through weakness, through our own deliberate fault,' but the word 'ignorance' was soon dropped and replaced by 'negligence.'

The Bible teaches that it is possible to sin through ignorance. For example, both Pharaoh and King Abimelech were counted guilty for taking Sarah into their harems, even though they were not aware she was Abraham's wife (Genesis 12, 20). Moses instituted a specific sacrifice to make atonement for those who had sinned unintentionally (Leviticus 4, Numbers 15.22–31). Elsewhere God explains to Ezekiel that those who have not been warned about their sin will still be punished for it (Ezekiel 33.6–8). In the New Testament, Jesus tells a parable about servants who are beaten despite the fact they do not know their master's will (Luke 12.48). Meanwhile, from the cross Jesus prayed forgiveness for his executioners, 'for they do not know what they are doing' (Luke 23.34; see also Acts 3.17, 1 Corinthians 2.8). It is thus legitimate to ask forgiveness for 'our sins of ignorance.'

Penitential Seasons

Lent is traditionally considered a period of fasting and penitence. In the early church it was a time of public penance and admonishment of notorious sinners, but later the whole Christian community began to observe the season. Advent too, as we await the arrival of Jesus our king and judge, is associated with penitence, although it has never acquired the rigorous disciplinary character of Lent.

The Anglican Reformers revised the traditional medieval devotions of Ash Wednesday into a penitential service entitled, 'A Commination, or denouncing of God's anger and judgements against sinners.' It is extremely stark, even by sixteenth-century standards, warning at length and in no uncertain terms of the terrible judgment of God upon sin and our need to repent without delay. Although some bishops wanted the Commination to be used at least four times a year, it never became popular and soon fell into obscurity. Alternative penitential services have now been produced and *New Patterns for Worship* provides a useful example (pp 396–401). Rites for Lent and Advent are also offered in *Lent, Holy Week, Easter* (1986) and *The Promise of his Glory* (1991) respectively, soon to be superseded by *Times and Seasons* (forthcoming, 2005).

Confession at the Occasional Offices

Baptisms best take place during main Sunday worship, of which confession is a normal part. Likewise marriages and funerals will usually include confession if they take place alongside Holy Communion. Yet what about marriages and funerals outside this context?

Although **weddings** are joyful occasions they can also be painful, both for those involved and their guests. The service is sometimes an unwitting reminder of broken relationships and wider family conflict. Therefore prayers of penitence may be appropriate. There is no reason, however, why this should particularly be the case for a service of dedication after a civil marriage or for the actual marriage of divorcees. Clergy who consider such ceremonies to be legitimate will have encouraged the couple in advance to repent of their part in the breakdown of a previous marriage. There is thus no need to repeat the exercise corporately, although general prayers of penitence may still be appropriate for other reasons. The recommended *Common Worship* confession is taken from a prophecy of Hosea, whose marriage to an adulterous wife led him to reflect on Israel's unfaithfulness and God's persistent love:

Lord our God,
in our sin we have avoided your call.
Our love for you is like a morning cloud,
like the dew that goes away early.
Have mercy on us;
deliver us from judgement;
bind up our wounds and revive us;
in Jesus Christ our Lord.
Amen.   based on Hosea 6

Likewise the absolution picks up the marriage theme:

The Lord forgive you your sin,
unite you in the love which took Christ to the cross,
and bring you in the Spirit to his wedding feast in heaven.

Funerals are unique as the one service for which the Anglican Reformers *decreased* rather than increased the penitential content. Partly because of belief in purgatory, there was a heavy emphasis in medieval burial rites on God's judgment and the terror of death. In contrast, Cranmer wanted Christian funerals to be celebratory, with an emphasis on the 'sure and certain hope' of resurrection to eternal life.[8] Nevertheless, confession of sin by those who remain may still be appropriate today within the funeral service and *Common Worship* introduces this option. Funerals bring us face to face with our own mortality and the fact that we will one day appear before God's judgment seat. They also sometimes remind us, poignantly, of missed opportunities and wasted years. In this context it is natural to repent of our sins and appeal to God's mercy, confident that Jesus' own death means we can be given a fresh start. Penitential prayers may be chosen to fit the theme of death and resurrection. One possible absolution, for instance, states:

> May God our Father forgive us our sins
> and bring us to the eternal joy of his kingdom,
> where dust and ashes have no dominion.

8

Symbolism

In the Old Testament penitence is often symbolized by an action, such as pulling out one's hair, rending one's clothes, weeping, fasting, wearing sackcloth or sitting in the dust. What symbolism, if any, is appropriate for the Christian penitent? What objects or actions might help us appreciate the reality of sin and the forgiveness of God? Many different symbols are now in use—some ancient, others recently invented by pioneers of 'alternative' worship. The following are amongst the most popular:

- **Posture** The attitude of our bodies sometimes reflects the attitude of our hearts (and indeed can form that attitude). In the Prayer Book, communicants are instructed to confess their sins while 'meekly kneeling' and this is still widely practised. However, in the Bible penitents adopt a variety of postures, such as standing (Nehemiah 9.2), sitting on the ground (Nehemiah 1.4), kneeling (Ezra 9.5) or lying prostrate (Ezra 10.1).

- **Light and darkness** In the Bible darkness is often a sign of God's judgment upon sin (for example, the noon-day eclipse during the crucifixion of Jesus) and light is a sign of God's presence and favour. Light also represents the holiness of God and the lamp by which he searches our hearts (Zephaniah 1.12). Therefore candles are lit for quiet reflection or the lighting turned low to encourage confession.

- **Water** sprinkled over the congregation as a symbol of cleansing.

- **Incense or aromatic oils** burnt as a symbol of purity.

- **Sign of the cross** made by all, as a symbol of their acceptance of God's forgiveness. Perhaps the congregation mingles, putting the sign of the cross on other people's palms or foreheads, with the words 'Because of the cross we are forgiven.'

- **'Liturgical colours'** Drab colours, like violet or blue, are traditionally a symbol of penitence.

- **Ash** imposed on foreheads on Ash Wednesday (although Jesus' warning in Matthew 6.16 may apply here).

- **Pictures** A series of penitential images is displayed (weeping, desert, slavery, exile and so forth) or a copy of a painting such as Rembrandt's *The Return of the Prodigal Son* or Zurbaran's *The Bound Lamb*.

- **Cross, stones, ribbons** A rough wooden cross is set up. Scarlet ribbons are pinned to the cross or stones left at its foot, to symbolize our sins forgiven through the death of Jesus.

- **Paper, sand, sea** Sins are written down on paper and burnt in a bucket or written in a sand-pit and then erased. For an outdoor service stones representing our sins are thrown into the sea or far away across the field.

- **Absence** The stark nature of penitence is emphasized by removing familiar decorations. For example, flowers or banners are taken away and the Lord's Table left completely bare. Music is restrained, played by a smaller worship band or with less frills by the organ. Absence was one of Cranmer's favourite penitential symbols.

Although Christians from a wide theological spectrum have begun to advocate such symbolism, extreme caution is needed. God looks on the heart not the outward symbol. He requires that we are humble not that we kneel, that we are penitent not that we have ash on our foreheads, that we rend our hearts not our garments (Joel 2.13). Furthermore, the use of objects and images in worship, especially if habitual, can be spiritually disastrous by leading us away from Christ instead of pointing us towards him. Partly for this reason the Anglican Reformers wisely reduced the level of ritualism they inherited from the medieval church. It is vital for congregations to know that we are forgiven and restored to relationship with God not by performing any symbolic ritual but by truly repenting of our sins and putting our faith in Jesus Christ alone.

9 Resources

In addition to *Common Worship* and *New Patterns for Worship*, useful penitential material may be found in:

Lent, Holy Week, Easter (London: SPCK/Church House Publishing, 1986)

The Promise of His Glory (London: Church House Publishing, 1991)

Enriching the Christian Year (London: SPCK/Alcuin Club, 1993)

Peter Graystone and Eileen Turner, *A Church for All Ages* (London: Scripture Union, 1993)

Eric Milner-White, *My God, My Glory* (1954; reissued London: Triangle, 1994)

Michael Perry (ed), *Church Family Worship* (London: Hodder & Stoughton, 1988)

Michael Perry, *Bible Prayers for Worship* (London: Marshall Pickering, 1997)

David Silk (ed), *In Penitence and Faith* (London: Mowbray, 1988)

Notes

1   James Packer, *A Passion for Holiness* (Nottingham: Crossway Books, 1992), pp 123–125.

2   See note 10 to the orders for Holy Communion, *Common Worship*, p 331.

3   Quoted in Mark Beach, *Using Common Worship: Holy Communion* (London: Church House Publishing /Praxis, 2000), p 34.

4   See further Andrew Atherstone, *'Search Me, O God': The Practice of Self-Examination*, Grove Spirituality booklet S 87 (Cambridge: Grove Books, 2003).

5   Francis Procter and Walter Frere, *A New History of the Book of Common Prayer with a Rationale of its Offices* (London: Macmillan, 1961 edition), p 370.

6   For the origins of many of these confessions, see Anne Dawtry and Carolyn Headley, 'A Service of the Word' in Paul Bradshaw (ed.), *A Companion to Common Worship* (London: SPCK/Alcuin Club, 2001), Vol 1 pp 80–81.

7   TW Drury, *Confession and Absolution: the Teaching of the Church of England, as Interpreted and Illustrated by the Writings of the Reformers of the Sixteenth Century* (London: Hodder & Stoughton, 1903). For a modern exposition of the reformed viewpoint, see John Stott, *Confess Your Sins: the Way of Reconciliation* (London: Hodder & Stoughton, 1964).

8   Geoffrey Rowell, *The Liturgy of Christian Burial: an Introductory Survey of the Historical Development of Christian Burial Rites* (London: Alcuin Club/SPCK, 1977).